# Diagnosis: Psychosis

## By Olivia Russo

For Anne (my mother)

Table of Contents

Foreword (October 2013)

Diagnosis: Psychosis

Difference

Before Psychosis

At My Worst

Recovering From Psychosis

Relapses and Ominous Relapses

Psychosis and Keeping Well

Acceptance

Afterword

# Foreword (October 2013)

I wrote this memoir in March 2012. Since then I've been deliberating over whether I actually wanted to have it published or if it was too personal to be published. However I know my message is powerful and that the audience it's really aimed at is the general public. The other reason I didn't send it off for publication straightaway was because, as you will see when you read on, most people I know (aside from close family and friends), have no clue I've suffered from psychosis. So it meant I would be revealing a lot and perhaps changing people's perceptions of me. I considered having my memoir published under a pseudonym, mostly because I know how strongly society stigmatises people who have suffered from mental illness, particularly psychosis. I spent many months wondering why I would subject myself to such stigmatisation. But there was another part of me that felt very proud of myself for writing this memoir and, of course, for having recovered from the illness and been well for years. I realised that if I didn't put my real name to this piece, I would in effect have been subject to criticism that I was then colluding with people who fail to see mental illness as just an illness, like any other illness is just an illness. I'm proud of my experience, tough as it was; I'm proud of my success story in recovering from psychosis (and writing this memoir helped me immensely); and I'm proud to be exemplifying that people who have suffered from psychosis are not "freaks", "possessed", "subhuman" or necessarily drug-users, that the general public think they may be. I'm Olivia Russo, an ordinary person. And I was as surprised as you might be that psychosis really can affect anyone, as it did me.

# Diagnosis: Psychosis

Most people haven't got a clue. They have no idea that the person they work with, socialise with, perhaps like, perhaps don't, spent two weeks of her life in a secure psychiatric unit. They have no idea my diagnosis was psychosis.

After my recovery and further recovery from relapses, I tended not to bother talking to people about my illness, or "episodes", because I found they simply did not understand. Or I found that when I talked about my problems, the person I was telling would only want to talk about theirs and, to be quite frank, I had enough of my own problems to contend with; I didn't need anyone else's. I was forgiving when this happened because I suppose they were trying to reach out to me and relate to what I was saying by them thinking, "We all have problems."

I couldn't help feeling though that they weren't really "getting" it; they didn't realise even to a minor degree what entirely losing touch with reality means. And how it meant that I had to relearn how to do everything, much like a baby has to learn to live in the world it has been thrown into. Only I was 20 years old and people were a little less forgiving when I found certain things (like boarding a bus) overwhelming. Of course a baby would never be expected to do something on its own but a grown woman, 20 years of age, is expected to be able to "just get on with it".

That tends to be the attitude towards a mentally ill person and it is usually a very good indicator that the person who thinks that has never had any real exposure to mental illness, either themselves or someone close to them. I think they are very fortunate to be in that position. However you'll notice a paradox here; I also think they are very unfortunate not to be able to understand what mental illness means.

Now I am well and can thankfully get on with my life; hold down a full-time job, run my flat and day- to-day living, I feel very fortunate to have experienced this illness. Nasty as it was, and ominous as it is (since I cannot be certain it will not haunt me again), it has given me a huge understanding, which I am only now realising in my late twenties, that most people do not have.

There are so many positives, as well as negatives, that have come from this illness. I will touch upon some as all of them might bore you. I will tell you exactly what it felt like to be psychotic, locked up, taken care of, and to get better. And then for it to come back again like a smack in the face, a number of times - too many for me to want to remember.

Out of all this the best thing has been the friends I now have. I have found I have things in common with people I might not otherwise have had a rapport with. Some of my friends know about my illness (although not in much detail) and a few, even some of my very closest friends, don't. People are unpredictable so I do not know if they would treat me differently if they did know but I would hope and guess they would not. And I hope they wouldn't prejudge me. The reason I haven't told them is because I have just never felt the need to tell them, as I have been quite well recently since they have been my friends. Why talk about something that isn't getting in the way of my life and risk friends letting it slip to other people who I would not want to know? This has happened in the past when friends I told took the liberty to tell others about my experience whilst I had thought I told them about it in confidence.

At the time though, when of course I could not hide the illness, since it was happening then, I lost some friends, usually because I had decided I did not want to have them as friends anymore because of their insensitive comments such as "I would have never let myself get that bad", as if I was to blame for my illness. Or, "I was ill once too but I got through it without any medication" to which these days I would respond, "Good for you; you obviously weren't anywhere near as ill as I was; that's really very lucky."

So I suppose you could say I learnt who my true friends are. And my closest friend, to whom I have dedicated this brief memoir and who I never had any doubt was my friend, is the greatest pal, carer and mother anyone could ever wish for – Anne. I love you mum, and would never have got where I am today if it wasn't for your love, support and belief in me. There's nothing I can say or do to repay you, not that you would want repayment of any kind anyhow. I'm not religious, and forgive me if you think I am being over-the-top, but I really mean it when I say, "Thank god for mum!"

# Difference

It's quite frightening being locked up, especially when no one tells you where you are. Before I explain the illness in more detail and the lead up to it, I want to give you just a glimpse of me at my worst. I had lost touch with reality so far that I did not know I was in a hospital and that I was ill; nobody told me. If they had, it might have been quite helpful and reduced my anxiety since I do recall thudding on the locked doors; yelling, screaming, saying all sorts - anything just to be able to get through those doors. In my paranoid state, I thought it was all a game. I really did. I thought I was supposed to do certain things in order to get out and that once I had, I would be presented with something like the job of my dreams, which at that time was to be a children's TV presenter (not something that I would enthuse about now but this was a time when Fearne Cotton was my absolute idol). This is why I gave my brand new, beautiful teddy bear, which my parents had bought for me when I was admitted, to the lady in the bed opposite me. I thought that kind act would result in me getting out. I have no idea where my logic for these scenarios came from. That's the thing with psychosis – because it is irrational and so inherently illogical, it simply cannot be explained in a logical way for other people to understand. It's no wonder then that they simply don't. I would go as far as to say that the majority of psychiatric professionals do not really understand psychosis either. I myself don't totally but I sure as hell have a greater understanding than anyone who has not experienced it him or herself.

And my understanding is also different from someone who experienced it because they took drugs since that is not, in my opinion, natural psychosis. How can it be? That is drug-induced. I was one of the very few (and by that I mean almost statistically insignificant) who ended up psychotic quite naturally. I have never smoked a "normal" cigarette let alone smoked cannabis or taken any other form of recreational drug. Stress (living in London and attending a top university) brought it about. This can be seen in two ways: either I am fascinating and "got it for free" as one psychiatrist put it to me; or I am unlucky in the sense that it is in me and not in a drug. It came from me and nowhere else. I am a positive thinker and so I opt to see it from the first perspective. I do think I am fascinating, which is why I have written this and you are reading it. I do not think I am any better or worse than anyone else and, by the same token, I do not think anyone else is better or worse than me. We are all just people who have experiences. It is by sharing those experiences and listening to what others say that we can learn to accept and embrace diversity – something that I care very deeply about.

I am different; we all are. Accept me, throw me in a psychiatric unit, listen to me, laugh at me – with me if you prefer. But the biggest issue most people face at some point in their lives is the realisation that anybody they have a problem with is not really who they have a problem with. This is because it is themselves who they are battling with and who they ultimately do not accept. It is only by accepting yourself that you can learn to accept other people. And once a person has realised this, they are more likely to embrace diversity.

I do believe I accept myself most of the time. I like myself, laugh at myself, and enjoy other people's differences. And most people do like me. After being ill and the illness shaking me, it took me a while to believe it but the best people in this world do like me. I feel like that's a great personal achievement.

To be brutally truthful though, I sometimes have moments of what I would call slight self-loathing. It's usually when I'm tired, stressed or embarrassed. I start to feel that, with my degree from the world-renowned London School of Economics University, I am something in between a joke and a failure for only being an admin assistant by the age of 28. Ask me ten years ago where I would be today and straight-A student me would have never said admin assistant.

But people do change and since I took on my job I have told people its title with pride. They look at me in disbelief at times and kind people say I am worth so much more than that, encouraging me to further myself. But I love my job and thoroughly enjoy working with my colleagues. It has taken a few jobs for me to find my feet and I think my lack of assertiveness in past jobs, and my unwillingness to accept compliments (since I did not have high self-esteem - a result of my illness), resulted in people thinking I really was as useless as I claimed to be. I suppose it was like a survival tactic. I didn't want people to think highly of me so that then I wouldn't have too much to live up to and then I would be less stressed and less likely to get ill again. I am still pretty bad at accepting praise and compliments. But I am confident, now, that the people I work with have faith and belief in me and that they value what I do. I am very fortunate indeed to be working in an environment where management is second-to-none, the work is interesting and I am never twiddling my thumbs. This combination is why I thrive in my job. And every day I am thankful that I am able to do it and am not mentally ill anymore.

Being mentally ill means in today's society that you will be stigmatised. You will be discriminated against and treated differently. Some people say the group that is most stigmatised in Britain is the elderly. No, actually the group just as stigmatised as the elderly is definitely the mentally infirm. I have a theory that if you are deemed to be not useful to working society then society is not interested in you. And it is that which is causing mentally ill people to be seen as outcasts. People look right down their nose at you if you have suffered from an illness like psychosis. It is simply (and disgustingly) acceptable for people to laugh at psychotic people and to think little of them. When I think about these facts, I feel we live in a disgraceful world. And a world that is going to be the biggest loser for it. I have given, and do give daily, a lot to the world. And I can relate to many things that other people can't even imagine. I suppose it's clear now why I do not tell people about my past psychotic illness. People would make assumptions that simply are not applicable.

I embrace difference and the difference that people like me make to the world. "Bring it on", is all I can say.

# Before Psychosis

I tend to see myself as pre-psychosis and post-psychosis because in many ways the illness has changed me greatly. My inherent character I suppose is much the same. But my outlook and take on things has been altered in such a way that I would describe I now have another lens to see life through.

Before I became ill, I took life very seriously from the age of about 10. Prior to that I had been fairly easy come, easy go. Secondary school then loomed and my big sister was no longer in the year above me at my school but in a year above me at the different, bigger, secondary school. And I thought, well I better start taking life seriously; I can't rely on Luisa anymore. I had to remember when a school reply letter needed to be signed and what was said in assembly. And I got my first pieces of homework, meaning I now had to think of school outside of school and it all seemed a bit grown up. So I decided to go along with it and take it all in as much of an adult way as possible, whereas up to the age of 10, I was a fan of gymnastics and the TV programme "Gladiators". I then hit 11 years of age, started secondary school and everything started to change. I remember on the inset day being confronted by a teacher in the playground for doing a cartwheel. He told me the students there don't do that. I looked at the boys running around playing football and couldn't fathom out why it was ok for boys to still play football but cartwheels for girls had to stop. Dutiful as ever, of course, I stopped practising gymnastics in the playground and limited myself to gym class where at least I was wearing my frumpy gym briefs.

I started taking my running more seriously. My dad would see me returning from a workout and encourage me all the more by telling me the person who comes second is the first loser. I was a child who took comments like that too seriously. However, it was all going quite well and by the age of 13 I was running cross country for Sussex. Not brilliantly might I add, more like modestly as, although I came first or second in my school's races, I was far beneath second place in those big races (sorry papa).

This became somewhat the story of my life, as it does for so many people. I did well in my small- scale community. Make that community larger and, relatively speaking, I had something to be proud of but nothing to speak of. It was a lesson I learnt again when I started university and my straight As had become modest 2:1s. First class honours from LSE were restricted for the incredibly intelligent people of the world. And by that I mean the people who just seem to have intelligence in every single one of their genes, rather than the average person whose intelligence inhabits their genes more mosaicly.

As you can see I had learnt this lesson before I became ill but I suppose there's always the determined belief that if you work harder you will do better. So when I breezed through my first year at university with three 2:1s and a 1:1, I thought, "Hey if I put some more effort in, I should be able to get my average up to a first", since that one module's first class honours (in my outside option, social psychology) had come as somewhat of a pleasant surprise.

And that's where it all went wrong. I cannot have regrets since if I hadn't pushed myself to do better, I would always be thinking, "Why didn't I?" And I can't blame it all on my determination to succeed as, in the year I got sick (my second year of university), I had a nocturnal and very inconsiderate roommate. The stress of determining to succeed added with very little sleep and the continual annoyance of the roommate who appeared to only care about herself, was the perfect recipe for disaster.

# At My Worst

On my first "episode" in February 2004 (during my second year at LSE), I seriously thought I had acquired a sixth sense. I had recently sat through a sociology of health and medicine lecture basically advocating that mental illnesses do not exist; they are a social myth (Thomas Szasz being the psychiatrist behind that ludicrous notion - see his book, "The Myth of Mental Illness" published by Harper & Row 1974). And so when I started to feel out of sorts, I went to a different lecturer's office to talk to him. The first thing I asked him was, "Do you believe in mental illness?" When he said yes, I walked right on into his office and sat myself down. His PhD student, who he had been talking to, looked on slightly dismayed and said she would come back later.

The conversation I had with this lecturer was mostly very serious, although with intervals of him laughing quite a lot and him making me laugh, as he could do so easily with many students. I was angry because I thought (falsely) that he had been mocking me in lectures and that he thought I was daft or something. Although I felt this way, oddly I also trusted him inherently.

Trust is the cornerstone to all social relationships in my opinion. Without trust, there may as well be no interaction since it would be quite meaningless without it. If friends breach my trust in them, I soon see them differently. Clearly this is also why I have not told many friends about my experience of psychosis because I don't want to risk losing them as I know this is what I'm like. So I keep them close without opening up to them about things too fragile in my mind to risk them disclosing to others.

So when my lecturer asked me why I had come to see him and not gone to my personal tutor (someone a student sees two to three times a year for five minutes) or the chaplain or a medical professional, I said quite without thinking, "Because I trust you." I would like to clarify here that this is a major statement for someone in the throes of paranoia to make. For a paranoiac to say they trust you, you must have a very good quality within you. And this guy was a decent, trustworthy person. I can usually tell the sort. His advice to me? "Go home.....and keep warm." The winter month was ice cold. He clearly thought I had overdone the studying a little bit, been traumatised by a guy (who wanted to date me but I wasn't sure of this guy's intentions) and that I just needed "home help" as he put it.

I did eventually get on a train home but not before I had stopped at my halls of residence to pick up a few things. I thought my lecturer had played a prank on me when I saw something for sale on a student's door. I have no idea why but I thought he was involved in that and that it was a joke directed at me. Then I went to my room and the lights were on (this freaked me out as no one was in the room but I of course now know it must have been me or my roommate who had left them on). I sensed there was a child hiding behind my bathroom door (it was too small a space for an adult so had to be a child). So I did not dare go in there. I wasn't going to let the spies get the better of me. As well as being spied on, I thought that my movements were being monitored. My roommate came home and I freaked the hell out of her with what I was saying and claiming. She was kind to me and walked me to the front of our halls and hugged me before I left. (She later told me she was scared shitless, emailed the lecturer I told her I had just spoken to and then asked a friend to stay in my bed all the while I was gone because she didn't want to be in the room alone.)

The twenty minute walk to Waterloo Station was even worse than my walk back from university. I was adamant there were now motorbikes following me and monitoring me or so I believed. I got to the station and felt that someone or something, anything that might have a recording device on it, was recording my every move. On the platform, a man was talking on his mobile phone. He gave me a sideways look whilst laughing and I was convinced he was jeering at me and about to monitor me on my journey.

On the train, it was crowded. I sat down amongst five others (it was one of those very old Southeastern trains). One woman was reading J K Rowling's "Harry Potter" and laughing intermittently. I thought she was mocking me for having liked Harry Potter. I wondered if she was a lecturer from LSE in disguise and putting me in my place. There was a young boy about five years of age sitting quietly, very quietly. His "acting" was almost too professional to be a child and I wondered if he was involved but did not realise it yet; a bit like a child who grows up in a religious cult and doesn't realise its significant until much later. A man behind me kept looking at me whenever I stood up, which I did fairly often because I wanted to know who was watching and to play them at their own game. He smiled a couple of times too and I thought he was making it obvious he was in on it. He was a good-looking, well-dressed, businessman aged about 35-40.

The train journey broke at Tonbridge, as it sometimes used to, and then we were to await the next connection. The smiling man got off and I was feeling and acting very confused, not knowing what to do. He did something weird. To this day I am not sure if it was creepy or loving, although at the time it felt comfortable. He put his cheek on mine and said in my ear, "If something awful has happened to you, I am really very sorry." His journey was over as this was his stop. He offered to buy me a coffee in a pub over the road and gave me his business card in case I changed my mind. (When I eventually got home, my mum found this card in my pocket and rang the man a few days later. They had a chat and he seemed genuinely concerned about me.)

But I wasn't home yet. And no one else was willing to talk to me to help me to get my train connection. People were deliberately avoiding making eye contact with me. I walked out of the train station and a taxi driver asked if I needed a lift. I presumed this was what I was meant to do and let him drive me back home, at a cost of £60. We laughed all the way home. I suppose the conversation must have been hilarious to him. But I also cried hysterically at one point and he stopped the car and said, "Do you want to go home to your parents like this?" I "sobered" up, would be a way to describe it (although I hadn't touched a drink) and got home. God knows what that taxi driver thought but he willingly took the £60 from my dad at the door. A few times, once I was well enough again, I offered to pay my parents back this vast amount (since to me, at that time, £60 was an awful lot of money). They refused it point blank and said I did the right thing to get in a taxi and get home safely.

Upon my arrival home via this taxi, my parents were baffled but convinced by my stories that I had psychotically invented in my head and made myself believe. I started crying uncontrollably and told them a student had hung himself because I turned him down on a date. I was dating an absolute weirdo at the time; a very intelligent but scary kind of a guy and mature student. I still wouldn't know what to make of him. But

I was distraught that he was now dead because of me. This I later learned was not true at all – my mother later spoke to the lecturer I first went to see, as he had given her his phone number, and he confirmed that the school would have heard if something like that had happened. I was so relieved.

But still my brain was doing weird things. I totally trusted it though – why wouldn't I trust my own brain that had never played tricks before? I was sleeping but not for long and I never felt rested. I now thought light bulbs were recording my movements. And when I got up in leisurely fashion one day, still not feeling rested, I went downstairs in my pyjamas and with my duvet to watch TV. I had never enjoyed TV so much in all my life! Everything was so relevant to me. And then it seemed the faces on TV were really looking directly at me and speaking to me. I was sure they could see me and at first was a little horrified that I hadn't done my hair and make-up. But the issues that they were dealing with were far more important and so I quickly dispelled that thought from my head.

I don't know where the day went or even days, how would I know? Night came and I went outside on a mission, just like all my movements were directed by some "mission". It was still freezing February weather and yet I went out in only my pyjamas and a pair of socks. I simply could not feel the temperature. My mother was horrified. But I explained to her that the lamp post at the top of our drive had a message on it and we went to read the graffiti basically; my mum only coming so as not to lose me and so that she could encourage me to come back into the house. Then my parents bolted the door by a bolt I had never seen used and so I did not know where it was on the door (up high, somewhere I had never thought to look). That was it; I was convinced the agencies had locked me in because I was becoming too hard to track down. And that's when I flipped.

I started screaming out of the windows and I pulled a kitchen cabinet door off to show my parents how serious it was that we were locked in. Because they were not scared to be locked in, I became convinced that they were in on it and not really my parents at all; never had been. My mum called an ambulance, knowing they could do no more. And when the sirens approached, I felt relief. I knew the ambulance was a safe place. But they turned up with the police as well and that unnerved me. The police were talking to my parents in the kitchen with one paramedic driver whilst the other paramedic sat with me. I was convinced she was really my godmother because she had blond hair and sounded like her or at least in my mind as I was by now hearing voices. My godmother's voice was amongst the ongoing commentary in my head but hers was a kind voice. So here I was now with her - my godmother paramedic who sat with me in my dining room saying, "Olivia! Olivia!" like she knew me. I was then sure she did and that she really was my godmother come to look after me.

I later learnt the two policemen and the ambulance paramedic driver were discussing with my parents how to admit me to hospital. The police were saying I could be taken to the police station and then forcibly admitted to hospital and the paramedic was saying if I agreed to go with the ambulance now voluntarily then the police wouldn't have to be involved at all. My dad was having none of the police's nonsense; for him there was no way I was going anywhere near a police station. And my mum explained to them that if she would be allowed to go with me then I would probably go to the hospital quite willingly. And the latter is what happened, although no one told me that was where I was heading (in my psychotic/symbolic mindset the ambulance looked more like a decoy than a vehicle transporting me to a hospital). Everyone gently coaxed and directed me to the ambulance, within which I kept seeing the driver's hands sticking out of the walls (I was hallucinating). It looked like a "stop" hand signal. But I wasn't going to stop. I was ranting away and putting the world right.

Then I got to A&E and my dad was there too (he had followed the ambulance with mum and I in it). We were waiting hours apparently. I remember waiting but didn't realise it was hours. My mum went to get hot chocolate and I was so scared of her drinking it, thinking it had been poisoned. (I still didn't realise this was a real medical place and a real A&E waiting room.) My parents and I went to a smaller room to wait and they were falling asleep, the night's activities having taken their toll. It was so quiet, I became convinced we were all dead and that this was heaven or hell. But I was pleased I still had my body and thoughts and would be able to write stories in this peace and quiet.

I stayed awake although my parents must have only been cat napping as they were quite concerned about me. Eventually a psychiatrist arrived. He was the spitting image of Andi Peters (or at least in my psychotic mind and with my ultimate ambition in life then to have been a children's TV presenter). I find it interesting to think though that he really may have been the spitting image of Andi Peters – how would I know now if I was hallucinating then or if that really was how he looked? Anyhow he was very calm and listened to me. I felt comfortable in his presence and he seemed to be in mine, which was refreshing. But then all of a sudden he'd signed a paper, passed it on and out the door he went. He had admitted me to hospital.

Then I remember being in another ambulance with my mum and this time two male paramedics; one sat in the back with us and the other drove. I was again setting the world straight. When no one paid any attention to me, I started yelling again but this time in Italian because I thought the paramedics hadn't understood my English so maybe they weren't actually English. Mum later said she had never heard me speak such fluent Italian.

The ambulance eventually pulled up and I walked into a brightly lit corridor, little did I know this was a hospital and that I was as ill as I was. Here I remained for two weeks. When I first set foot on the ward, I thought it was another mission to be carried out. I believed everyone was acting. It wasn't until I started taking medication and sleeping, and my mum told me I was in a hospital, that I realised these people were nurses and patients and I was as ill as some of the patients, if not more so.

But initially it took a lot to make me take the medication voluntarily. My father had always said you shouldn't take medication you don't need. (He still rather strangely only very rarely takes half a paracetamol for any pain.) And as far as I could see, I didn't need any medication so that wasn't going down my throat. The nurse and my mum battled and battled with me verbally to take it but I would not. It came very close to me having to be forcibly given it (probably via an injection). But thankfully, I eventually agreed to take it. Apparently I was saying things like, "It's ok mum; I've got enough to write my book now." (Ever since primary school I have wanted to write a book.) And although she knew I was dreadfully ill, mum later told me that at this moment a thought crossed her mind that it was actually a game to me and I was not really ill at all – wishful thinking I suppose you could say.

The medication (anti-psychotics, olanzapine) kicks in usually as soon as it's taken. But on my first psychotic episode it took a while to take effect and the nurses in the psychiatric unit were quite surprised when I kept getting up off the sofa (where they were initially trying to rest me) on a mission to determine something. My psychosis was so far gone that even the medication had to fight with it. Once the medication (a dose of 20mg of olanzapine, I am told) did settle me I slept for 17 hours straight, before being forcibly woken by a nurse who kept rubbing and slapping my arm and telling me to open my eyes. Eventually I opened one eye and saw her looking down at me. She held my arm, smiled and said, "God bless you dear." Then left me alone. Great, I thought, "Another five minutes." Then I was woken again and there were many nurses around the bed. Taking my temperature is what I remember, but they must have been monitoring other things. I was crying, calmly and despondently, whining really. I didn't know what was going on.

Then of course it's medication, medication, medication. And boy does that knock you back! Even getting up to wash my face felt like a mission. My limbs were so heavy. Things like reading a paragraph in a newspaper were nigh on impossible. My concentration was zapped.

And I just could not stop sleeping. I remember rubbing my eyes one day when my parents were visiting and I felt my eyelashes. I was so thankful to still have them because the last time I wiped my eyes (as I often do when I'm not wearing make-up) I couldn't feel them. I had presumed the nurses had cut them off and I thought to myself, "They've even cut off my eyelashes, the bastards." But when I later felt them I was so happy and exclaimed, "Oh I've still got my eyelashes! I thought they'd cut them off to make me see sense." My parents fell about laughing at what I hadn't intended as a joke. And when my relatives rang my parents later that evening to see how I was doing, mum recounted this event to them and they all agreed I would be fine, it was just a matter of time. The thing is, I was genuinely relieved and grateful to still have my eyelashes as I had felt them earlier and they were not there (obviously at that time I must have been hallucinating).

My parents visited every day. When they told me the date one day, I could not believe it was a week later than I thought. I was stuck in the week before and my haziness prevented me from keeping up with what day and time it was. I thought they were having me on, to make me stay in the hospital a week longer or something but they convinced me that what they had said was the truth.

My sister came to see me (she travelled from Egham to Eastbourne and back in a day because I had been asking after her). She was in the middle of her last year at university and was busy with revision and coursework. But she told mum that I was her priority and if I was asking after her then she was coming straightaway. I had indeed been asking after her. I thought, because I hadn't seen her for so long, and since being in hospital, that something had happened to her as well. I even thought she had been taken away from me and was no longer going to be my sister. So I carried a photo of her around with me in hospital. I had it in my jogging suit pocket by day and in my pyjama top pocket by night. Nobody was taking Luisa away from me. I showed her photo to all the nurses and made it clear, "This is Luisa; she's my sister." They said that was nice. So when Luisa arrived and was perfectly fine, again I felt huge relief. I didn't have much energy to chat but her visit soothed my soul to no end and aided me in my recovery from all the confusion going on in my head.

Adding to this confusion was the fact that the nurses didn't wear uniforms which made it all the more difficult to decipher who was who, i.e. who was a patient and who was a medical professional. I was permitted day release (by a smart psychiatrist) and was instructed to ask a nurse for permission. I asked a few people if they were nurses before I got to one who actually was one.

# Recovering From Psychosis

I had a week of day releases where I had to go back to hospital each night to sleep. Even though I was a voluntary patient, it still felt a bit like going back to a sort of "prison" because the doors were locked. Mum came to get me each day and returned me to hospital each night. We played Annie's "Tomorrow" on each return car journey back to hospital. Now I can't listen to that song without memories of this time. But I feel it is a happy song and optimistic so, although it reminds me of this time, I do enjoy hearing it.

I know I wasn't back to my old self when I was permitted day release. But the crucial point was I wasn't a danger to myself or to anyone else. In fact the nurses quickly realised I didn't really need to be in the secure part of the psychiatric unit but there were no other beds available at the time so I had to stay there.

My first trip home was a bit uneventful after having been so psychotic. There were no television crews waiting to film me or university lecturers wanting to discuss my future as I still psychotically wondered if there might be. It was just quiet old home. And, after the commotion and noise of the psychiatric unit, boy was it peaceful. No one here was talking nonsense like some of the patients at hospital were and I of course no doubt had been.

Real reality was like a "coming to". It took time but within days I was able to realise that what I had been thinking wasn't actually real. There was no conspiracy against me and nobody was "out to get me".

Each day when I returned home, I would have a bath (a luxury you can't really enjoy properly in hospital) and I would watch the TV programme "Richard & Judy" with mum whilst she also made the dinner. I opened my post. Relatives had sent get well cards and also get well gifts, which I remember were a sports vest for dancing, a silver bracelet and two key ring teddy bears (two cousins had had the same idea).

I was pleased with these thoughtful gifts and so thankful to be home with the likelihood of coming home permanently being imminent (a week later). But something in me had gone. It was like the candle that had been shining inside me all my life had been blown out by a violent gust of cold wind. I felt empty, lethargic and heavy (the medication does this). And I had no idea of the misery that was to come. Little did I know how long it takes to recover from psychosis and how long I would have to take the damn medication.

My daily dose of olanzapine was reduced from 20mg in hospital to 15mg once I was home then to 10mg. I remained on 10mg for many weeks (probably two to three months). Then it was reduced to 5mg then 2.5mg and eventually, after about six months in total, I came off it altogether. But I was miserable. It had sucked out my soul. Yes it stopped the psychosis but it also dried me up, literally too as my periods ceased the whole time I was on it. I didn't feel like a person – I was supposed to be a grown woman but without my periods anymore, and knowing I wasn't a man or a child, what was I then? I'd had to defer my year at university so my student status was also on hold.

My reader can probably tell from the sombre tone of my writing, that recovering from psychosis during these six months made me feel depressed. So in effect, I became ill on top of already being ill. I was surprised how no medical professional batted an eyelid when I told them I was feeling depressed. It would seem that was part and parcel of the ordeal (and again perhaps it was the attitude of "just get on with it").

But it was a new feeling to me. I had always been so full of zest for life and optimistic about the future, hopeful about opportunities. Now I felt low and hopeless. My godmother rang to see how I was and I said, quite truthfully, "It's like my whole life has been taken away from me." She gasped and said, "Olivia! That is a bit of an exaggeration!" But, like I say, it was the brutal truth of how I was feeling. I had gone from being an enthusiastic LSE student in the heart of London, going to the theatre most weeks and dancing and going to the gym, to suddenly having a life that now involved my bed and medication plus a little bit of food for the sake of survival (I had lost my appetite on the medication; a lucky side effect since the opposite has happened to other people who have been on it and have unfortunately ballooned in weight).

My mum kept my spirits up well enough for me to look forward to her returning from work each day and then later tucking me into bed (a 20 year old needing her mother to tuck her in). She reassured me that I would be ok again; it was just a matter of time and that if I took my medication, as I had been instructed to do so, and listened to the doctors and nurses, then it would just be this one-off "brief psychotic episode" and I'd be very unlikely to suffer from anything like that again.

Because that is what the psychiatrists kept on telling us. They kept saying how statistically insignificant the chances of relapse were and how surprised they were that it had come about without the use of recreational drugs in the first place. I forget the amount of times the psychiatrists asked if I had ever smoked marijuana. It annoyed me because it felt like they hadn't been reading my file before seeing me because, if they had, they would have seen that I had said time and time again that I had never smoked marijuana and would never have any wish to. But still they felt it necessary to advise me not to try it, advice which seemed odd given the amount of times I had reiterated that it had never, and would never, interest me.

I believed the psychiatrists when they said how unlikely, almost impossible, it would be for me to get ill with psychosis again. And I used that knowledge to will myself better on my road to recovery. It gave me something worth looking forward to. I thought of this each day.

Then of course it would be time to take my daily dose of medication and I would be knocked backwards again. It felt a bit like a sedative that physically had the effect of going straight to my back, making me sleepy and knocking me out. Then the next day around 7pm usually, just when I was starting to feel myself again (i.e. a little bit enthusiastic about life), it would be time to take the next dose.

But I didn't give up. I was going to get better. The psychiatrists told me so and I believed them. My mum kept telling me too and reminded me when I was feeling low that at least it wouldn't come back. I remember when I was feeling in better moods, we would play lots of card and board games. They were great in helping me to concentrate again, in a fun way. They teased and focused my brain and the activity made me feel that I could still achieve; even losing a game meant that I had still got through it.

Imagine how I felt then, when I returned to university the next academic year, did well and then reached my third year, for the psychosis to smack me in the face again. What was it every psychiatrist had told me?

# Relapses and Ominous Relapses

I sometimes forget the order the relapses happened in and how many I've had. I know the first relapse (at Christmas time in my third year of university) involved depression. The diagnosis was "depression with mild psychotic symptoms". I know the psychotic symptoms were a little more than I was letting on but I was fearful of being admitted to hospital again so didn't voice my psychotic feelings too loudly. I was now savvy with hindsight and still fearful of hospital. Going into hospital again was never on the cards but I didn't know that at the time and I did not want to go back or have too much of a "psychotic" label.

When the psychiatrist (who came to see me at home) asked if I felt depressed, I burst into tears. I had been tearful for the past few days. It was uncontrollable, like vomiting tears. I had to keep swallowing hard not to blubber too much in public. Anything could set me off – seeing sunlight on a rooftop, watching someone texting on their phone. And it was like I felt I could feel other people's pain. But of course I was psychotic too. However I was relieved when the psychiatrist placed the emphasis on depression rather than psychosis. Depression is still socially unacceptable according to the society we live in but I'd learnt psychosis is more unacceptable to that same society.

I was prescribed anti-depressants and olanzapine: the combination made me ravenous with hunger. But I was soon allowed to come off the olanzapine – too soon, I should say, as I know I wasn't stable enough to come off it but at the time I trusted the doctors knew best, even though I had the knowledge that I had downplayed my symptoms, I still thought the doctors were the experts, not me. I remained on the anti-depressants for months. (When I eventually came off them - after university when I had started working life - I had to take two days off work because I was so dizzy I couldn't leave my bed.) Anti-depressants work for some people and for others they have no effect. They did not ease my depression in the slightest. But at the time they did stop me feeling tearful at the most ridiculous of things.

After this "episode", I returned from the university Christmas holiday (2005) to complete my university course and my final year. It was a year of feeling "on edge". I was paranoid but also aware that tutors knew a bit more about me and might have just been treating me like that, which could have made me feel that way (a bit like a self-fulfilling prophecy). I still do not know which.

I sat my final exams. I knew I had to just get through them but for one exam I was not fit to be there. However if I didn't sit it then I would have had to re-sit it the next summer, which seemed impossible – I couldn't remain at university any longer. I sat the exam feeling paranoid throughout. The examiners must have taken an average of my year's work for that module as my paper was a disaster but my mark was ok. During the exam I had been so anxious that I was dehydrated. Memories of being 20 blocks away on 11th September 2001 seemed to be haunting me that day and I became convinced that there was a bomb in one of the students' bags in the corner of the exam room. Which one I didn't know but I "felt" it was there. A reasonable reaction to an experience I had had at the age of 18 but why was it haunting me then and there, aged 21? It was because I was psychotic again.

I left the exam room when the three hours were up, feeling dehydrated and psychotic, knowing my paper had been crap and I walked straight out onto Aldwych into an oncoming car. It stopped just in time. I felt no fear. I knew I was ill again and felt my world was falling apart like deja vu, so why care about anything?

Strangely I was hungry (previously psychosis had dispelled hunger pangs but this time I was feeling, "To hell with it, if I'm psychotic again!") and so I sat in Pret a Manger eating a tomato, basil and mozzarella baguette. Someone next to me turned and nudged my arm as they did so, then they apologised. I didn't know if they were "in on something". I had this thought and then decided, what do I care if they are?

With the help of one of my cousins who worked in London and came to fetch me, I went home to my doctor who shouted at me for having gone up to London to take that exam. I took his lecture and accepted it. But I was also pleased I had sat through that exam, that I only had one more exam to go and that I didn't even care what the result would now be. My doctor put me back on olanzapine.

I took my very final exam whilst on a fairly high dose of medication and, surprisingly, I managed to answer all three questions in the exam time and I passed with a good mark considering (and with no allowances, a doctor's certificate didn't interest me – a simple pass would have sufficed). Overall, I managed to obtain a 2:1 (Hons) BSc Sociology degree and I definitely deserved it. My third year results were the worst of the lot but I had done so well in my first and second years that the overall mark worked out well (added to this my third year results were still mostly average so certainly not failures). Many students obtained their better marks in their first and second years and I was one of them but I had also battled with a very frightening disease throughout most of my time at university and, in my opinion, I had topped every leader board. I was fast developing a two fingers-up approach to the world that kept getting me down. This new approach helped me fight the psychosis that I was determined would not beat me.

Yes, it came back again. I've relapsed once since my university days. Interestingly, this was very early on in my working life where the management was disappointing and I dreaded going in every day. That's why I am so relieved to have a job in a wonderful department, where management is very supportive (even without me having told them about my past illness). Good management has made all the difference. And it has helped me learn how I work best and what I want from life.

A high-flying career that impresses other people does not interest me. I wonder if it really interests those who go for it themselves or if it's just the adulation they enjoy rather than the job. I'm sure some people at the top are very happy there but I would bet the majority isn't.

I have been forced to rein in my ambitions in life, to not strive too high or do anything too stressful. As frustrating as this was at first to accept, it's actually helped me a great deal. It may have helped in preventing me relapsing and it's given me other priorities in life to focus on. My very active social life means a lot to me and it's social activities that make me happy (i.e. dancing, going to the theatre and seeing my many friends a lot). It's meant that I have the courage to point blank refuse to do anything just to "go along with the crowd" (i.e. drinking/clubbing, which never appealed to me anyway) as I simply do not have the energy for the stress of all that.

People don't always understand but, with my altered approach to the world we live in, I don't really give a damn about that. People are forever telling me I could do so much more with my life, especially those who knew me in my school years. And yes I know I could. But I can't be bothered to get there if getting there possibly means getting ill.

I can't expect people who have no idea of my (hopefully past) illness to understand why I am not ambitious like most young people. And it can feel tricky when they ask me questions about future career plans but I answer in as honest a way as possible (without disclosing health issues) and if they remain perplexed, I couldn't care less.

You see, the threat of this illness does remain and I need to take it seriously because I don't want a lifetime of relapses. I want a lifetime of contentment and health because that's what success is.

# Psychosis and Keeping Well

Living with psychosis is difficult to describe. I can explain why. Psychosis is a false reality, one that the person suffering from the disease believes as if it were a reality. Put another way, it is reality for them. Thankfully this is not my normal state of mind. Here are examples of how I feel when I feel a relapse approaching. I need to remember these feelings in order to prevent further relapses. I've been successful in this mindset for a few years now as I haven't suffered a relapse for a very long time.

I remember after my third or fourth relapse, my doctor saying I had to know the difference between reality and psychosis. I got frustrated and asked, "*How*? How do you know what you are thinking is not real? What you are seeing is not there? How do you *know*?" He shrugged his shoulders gently and delicately put it to me, "You *have* to know."

But if psychosis is to be taken for what it is (as just described), it needs to be understood that it is impossible for a psychotic person, whose brain is telling them one thing, to be able to make their brain tell them something else. It is not humanly possible for a person to control their brain in this way.

However Dr John Nash (the amazing academic and Nobel Prize winner who suffered from schizophrenia) learnt to see his attempts at controlling his psychosis as a sort of "diet". He actively sought to stop his brain from indulging in psychotic thought and yet it was a struggle much like a diet is. But it works to an extent and I suppose that is what my doctor was getting at. You have to train yourself to think otherwise; you have to be careful not to let it run away with you.

This is possible but it certainly is easier said than done. I do not dismiss its usefulness in keeping the illness at bay but I do also understand the very real nature of psychosis because I've felt and experienced it.

How to describe what psychosis feels like? Well, in my experience, things look sharper, people's eyes look sinister, their voices sound different, and their breath can smell not unpleasant but like a smell you've never smelt on someone before (weird). I believed people in my life were the "real" famous people and the ones we see on the television are just their doubles who do the TV work for them. For example I was convinced my mum was Germaine Greer (odd seeing as she isn't even a feminist) and at one point my dad was the Pope (again, odd seeing as he isn't even religious). And as you know, the very first psychiatrist to see me in A & E (when he eventually turned up) as far as I was concerned was the "real" Andi Peters. I even told him this and when he kept a straight face, I knew I had to be right.

I remember every sound being amplified and meaning something. A tapping sound was like a tape recorder going on or off, taping me. A helicopter sound in the sky was like a tracking device to me and it was recording my every movement. And any person's comment or glance had some meaning to me even if they themselves were unaware of it. That last one's hard to explain.

People think if you are paranoid then you're likely to think people are talking about you, bitching about you or have some conspiracy theory against you. And that is true. A paranoid person may well feel that way and I have felt it myself. But for me, there was more to it than that. When I was feeling very paranoid, I felt that there were people "involved" in a conspiracy against me but some of them didn't actively know it. For example if a child or even a cat looked at me, I knew they would not have the knowledge to understand the conspiracy they were involved in but them being there, at that place, at that time, was some kind of control by an adult who put them there to maybe spy on me or put me off-guard. This feeling only really occurred when I was very psychotic, i.e. the first time, which was when I had not been able to spot any warning signs beforehand to enable me to "nip it in the bud" before I became more ill. The reason I couldn't do this was of course because I didn't know what I was thinking was wrong (as ridiculous as that may sound to you and even sounds to me now I am well). Neither did I know that I was ill, whereas with a relapse (second time onwards) the sufferer is more insightful of the disease's symptoms.

During relapses I often felt like the world was "getting at me". This first started at university, although I have to say I felt a bit like this at school in adolescence too. For example thinking that teachers were talking about me. However, teachers do talk about their pupils in the staff room and I know I was of a very studious nature with a slightly cocky side to me, as one teacher would often describe me. (Since the illness, this confidence has been knocked with a sledge hammer but gradually I have found myself to have the confidence to be humorous again as that was all it was.) But I wasn't delusional at school. And one of my peers even told me her family talked about me at their dinner table. Her mother was a teacher and taught both of us.

However the delusional "getting at me" is far more sinister than that. It can feel like the world is out to get you, that there is no way out, nowhere to hide and nowhere for you to find peace. It can feel like you're being "set up" or "dropped in it". Or it can just feel like other people are playing a game with you. I even thought this of the nurses who came to visit me when I was home from university having suffered a relapse. They would change shifts and it seemed to be a different nurse visiting me each time. I told them I thought they were playing a game with me and, credit where it's due, they ensured the same nurse visited me each time from there on during my recovery from that relapse. Added to this, the nurse had the same name as one of my god-sisters and that seemed to comfort me at the time.

Back at university, during further relapses, if I saw two lecturers talking and one of them was looking my way, I would think it was about me and they were laughing at me. Then walking down the corridor in between lectures, the commotion would be kind of amplified but somehow distant from me. And students would pass me saying things like "books, books" and it would seem they were referring to my determination (alongside so many other students) to have the correct books for that week. And it felt like they were mocking me. In hindsight now, I find it easy to disentangle most of my psychotic thoughts and behaviour and see them as an illness. But some things were so vivid and of course there is the very real likelihood that much of what I saw and heard was happening. But my take on it (perhaps my thoughts on what was said or happening) was wrong.

These days keeping well is my ambition in life. And I am achieving it every day. Long may that success continue! If I relapse again, I will refuse to let it get me down because I am living proof that I know how to get better again. I know how to nip it in the bud now. It's just an illness, like some people have high blood pressure. No big deal for me. The big deal seems to be what society thinks of it – more on that later.

It took me till my late twenties to realise that perfection is actually being healthy. Any other form of perfection is quite unhealthy and usually very momentary. That is why I like to read success stories of people who have overcome things or learnt to control them, conditions like eating disorders or depression or Tourette's syndrome. I love the autobiographical form of writing and find it empowers both the author and their reader. Weaknesses are usually hidden strengths. If you can learn from other people's as well as your own then you have more of a chance of accepting people as different and seeing yourself as a valuable individual too. I've found this to be really helpful for me and it's boosted my self-esteem since getting ill.

Being able to get by in life by my standards has led to me feeling very empowered. I try to live my life according to what I value and not what other people think is right for me. Let's face it; most of them don't really know me very well anyway. And they don't need to.

I feel so lucky to have a personal nurse at hand whenever I need her and that's my mum. She's a big part of me being able to stay well. I also visit my doctor regularly and find I come away feeling uplifted. He understands the illness better than other doctors (in the past when I saw a different one as it was my doctor's day off, she asked me how much medication she should prescribe me. I was horrified and thought, "For goodness sake, you're the doctor!"). My doctor has thankfully had training in mental health. Many general practitioner doctors haven't. Isn't that ridiculous? It's a bit like not learning about legs. What doctor would dream of not learning about legs? No wonder mental health is brushed under the carpet when even the medical profession itself doesn't see it as vital. I am my own best doctor and do believe I know better than most medical professionals. Remember all those psychiatrists who wouldn't accept I hadn't taken drugs? Who said there would be no relapses? Is it any wonder I listen mostly to myself these days?

I will say though that this illness feels very much in the past. It's only a threat that it might come back and if it does, I am ready for it and so it will never haunt me as badly as it used to. And I am now very aware of what psychosis is. Having been psychotic, I have a new way of seeing things and it has become a small part of me in a way, if only because of the understanding I now have, which other people are not as privileged to ever have. However psychosis is just a slight bleed when the scab on my brain gets knocked. It doesn't rule my life. It is just a lens I can see things through and it's helped make me who I am today. I've always been a good person. Since this illness I feel I am also a much more understanding person.

# Acceptance

I totally accept that the reality my psychosis created wasn't real. Some people who have suffered from psychosis unfortunately do not reach the stage of realising this so I feel very lucky that I can definitely see it for what it was – just an illness. Getting better each time with medication was like gradually having my perception focused; much like an optician focuses a person's eyesight with the glasses they prescribe. Once it's focused you realise what nonsense you were seeing before as compared to what is really there.

Just an illness then, but for some reason society still ridicules a mentally ill person. Most stigmatised groups' rights have been well fought for in the majority of western cultures. For example, ethnic minorities are having their voice heard, as are gay communities, and people living with debilitating conditions like a physically life-threatening illness. But you rarely hear of people sticking up for mentally ill people's rights. It does feel like society believes they don't really matter.

For example, I know whenever I'm asked to sponsor a friend or colleague for a charity event they are a part of, it will always be for a socially acceptable cause like cancer, The British Heart Foundation, or a children's hospital. And that is great; it really is. But I feel saddened that it is so rarely for a charity like Mind. And I can honestly say I have never even seen a person collecting charity money outside a supermarket for a cause relating to mental illness. Sadder still, no fund- raising charity would advertise its fundraising slogan mentioning a condition like schizophrenia, which is an illness that is likely to greatly reduce a person's life span (no doubt this may be related to the lack of support they receive in our society).

This is what I was getting at earlier; society will be the biggest loser for this attitude. And I will not apologise for my preaching now as it needs to be said. People jeer at what they do not understand. They do not understand because they are not taught and do not want to hear about it. This ignorance breeds discrimination, which re-ignites the us/them dichotomy between people who do not suffer from mental illness and those who do. Because mental illness is seen as socially unacceptable, this discrimination is not frowned upon and, tragically in many cases, mentally ill people become downtrodden.

It is human nature to compartmentalise and pigeon-hole people. This is something our society should be fighting against because we are all individuals with different experiences needing to be shared for us to understand each other better. By silencing valuable people, society is quite clearly missing out.

So I've told my account of mental illness. It was a trauma I never thought I would endure and that taught me a lot about my previous attitudes. I've conveyed my psychosis to you and I hope now if you hear of a person who has suffered from mental illness, you do not think of the tabloid press's notion of a violent person. It's amazing what some people will believe. The truth is most mentally ill people are not violent.

To reiterate then: the fact of the matter is mental illness is like any other illness. It's just a person's weakness like any physical illness might be a person's weakness. And most people can laugh about their weaknesses. I want to finish this small chapter with a smile about mental illness. I remember when I first got ill; it was months before I felt like myself. One day after a joke, my mum said to me how good it had been to hear me laugh, that she hadn't heard me laugh in a long time. And I realised then how long it had been since I'd laughed at all. I think it helped mum to see I was nearing recovery then. And it made me realise how important seeing the funny side is.

You see I remember, from the psychiatric unit, things like a woman who walked around with a comb stuck in her hair like she had got waylaid whilst combing it. And another patient who kept saying she had to be at the police station at 10am (I now realise this may well have been the case but I didn't realise that then). And early on in my stay, I thought I wasn't a patient at all and so I started to help the nurses to care for the others (kindly, the nurses thanked me). Another day, when I had refused my medication the night before (I do not even remember doing this but apparently I had) I started to find the place hilarious to the extent that I was asking nurses, in between hysterical laughter, how they managed to keep a straight face in that place. I also managed to set another patient off with laughter, as laughter can be contagious in that way!

I mean you have to see the funny side. Beneath all the crap that mental illness gives you, there are glimpses of hilarity in amongst it. If only society could embrace it, see what it is missing and laugh about mental illness with us rather than at us as inferior beings.

# Afterword

Most writers thank whom they want to at the beginning of their work. To me, that is ridiculous. You will remember that I did dedicate my writing to my mother very early on and that's because I want her to stand out as the rock of everything in my life. And I wanted to introduce her to you as early as possible.

But I left thanking other people till now because I feel a thank you is necessary once someone has done something for you and in this case, you have read my memoir and hopefully understood its message. And for that I thank you.

During my illness, my family was very supportive, extended family included (two cousins in particular were always on standby when I needed them). My sister has been supporting me for years in talking things through with me and, rather bluntly sometimes, putting things into perspective. That kind of approach to it all has really aided my recovery and helped me to see the illness for what it is and nothing more. I want to thank her. And also my father for visiting me in hospital, which I don't think was the easiest thing he's ever done. And for accepting when things became too much for me each time I relapsed. My extended family has sought to understand and allowed me to talk to them at any time. Some of them travelled a long way to visit me for a very short time in hospital. It was a moment when I realised the true meaning of "making my day".

I would like to thank my doctor, who may prefer not to be named. He has been supportive right from the beginning. I usually leave my doctor's appointments with a smile on my face (and one on his) with some gentle words and good advice to take away with me. Thank you doctor. Not many people can say they enjoy going to see their doctor, but I can.

I would especially like to thank all of the mental health nurses who attended to me in hospital and in, what's termed as, "the community" (i.e. once I was home from hospital). They really took the time to talk to me and advise me, even when I was talking nonsense. They watched me progress each day and gave realistic praise and encouragement. I found them optimistic in their approach and very caring in their manner. It sometimes seemed the nurses knew much more about my condition than the psychiatrists did, although my doctor has corrected me in saying that the nurses had more *time* than the psychiatrists did. Well if that's so then "time is a great healer" and so are nurses.

The best nurse of all is the one who's probably given me too much time but a perfect amount when I needed it most. Yes mum, it's you again. And I thank any carer who nurses a loved one the way my mum supports me. You're the reason we survive.

Printed in Great Britain
by Amazon